STORY SEEDS

52+ Ideas and Prompts for Sci-Fi and Fantasy Writers to Get Their Next Story Written NOW

By

Shandee Niswander

Copyright © 2019

www.NisFreelance.com

For my fellow writers,

You inspire me every day with your creativity as you make a mundane world more interesting.

A big thank you to my friends and beta readers who helped quality check this book:

Chris McGill

Andy Z

Michael J

Legal Disclaimers

Parts of this book may be reproduced for educational purposes
in a creative writing class setting.

No part of this book may be reproduced for monetary gain
or copied into other resources
without permission from the author.

Cover art is an Unsplash provided zero commons image

by Yeshi Kangrang

Nis Freelance
Content Accelerator Series

Story Seeds

Sci-Fi and Fantasy Edition

52+ Ideas and Prompts
for Sci-Fi and Fantasy Writers
to Get Their Next Story
Written NOW

Shandee Niswander

Introduction

It's that time again. Maybe you have a creative assignment due. Maybe the 30-day writing challenge is close at hand. Perhaps you have a driving itch to write a story, but you do not know what!

I created this book as a brainstorming reference for all writers in the sci-fi and fantasy genres. As a writing coach and ghostwriter, I often see new authors who want to write a story, but they feel lost on their starting point. This book and others that follow are my way of helping those who just need that spark to get their creative juices flowing.

I modeled this book after a creative writing class assignment. We had just finished reading "The Lady or the Tiger" with its famous cliffhanger ending. We were all tasked with analyzing the story and writing out what we thought happened next. I'll never forget how fascinating I found it that 27 people had two possible outcomes, but they still created 27 unique endings.

Despite the fun and thrill of sharing those endings, there was a distinct flaw. We were all tasked with writing an arena setting. With the same doors. The same choices. While each story was certainly unique in execution- none of us could take our stories and submit them to a contest or publish them. None of them were so unique that we could use them outside of a fan fiction platform or among friends. It was just a fun exercise.

I noticed a great deal of prompt books have a similar issue- they give you a great idea. But it is set within a very small boundary- one that shows a very distinct theme for everyone who uses it. When I set out to make a prompt book- I wanted to give you more than that. I wanted you to have the option to publish your hard work if you saw fit. And with that in mind, I created my first Story Seed reference for my fellow writers.

With that in mind, there are a few important things to cover before we get started.

This book will not tell you what to write.

The main goal of the book is to spark your unique ideas. If you give the same prompt to ten people, you will get ten distinctly different stories. All with their own plot, characters, conflicts and themes. Some will be short stories. Some will write novels. Some writers will use it as a starting point in a whole world-building campaign. And the unique magic? All ten writers could submit their final work to the same publisher or contest without fear of sounding too similar.

Why? Because the situations that make up the seed are very open. Every writer will have their own idea of what a 'monster' or 'crisis' or 'secret' will be. It doesn't limit the physical setting or the type of protagonist. It does not limit your end goals or types of conflicts. The prompt is a spark. And it's up to the writer to turn that spark into a flame.

Don't worry! If you need an extra boost, there are at least five developing questions attached to each seed to help you fine tune the idea into your unique creation.

This book will not tell you how to write.

This book is purely and completely for brainstorming. There is no filler, or steps to develop those brainstorms. It is made specifically for the brainstorming stage.

I'll offer up future works about world building, plot development, and other topics in the future. I'm not leaving you stranded though! You will find a handy list of recommended tools and readings at the end of the book.

How to Use This Book

There are 52 basic prompts, and each one has five or more guiding questions. You can use just the prompt, or you can use the questions to develop it further.

If you are a daily exercise writer, you could use each prompt as a weekly theme and each guiding question as a daily focus.

If you are an instructor or lead a writing club, I would be thrilled to know the prompts were used. Let me know how it goes!

If you are writing short stories or novels, you have enough prompts to do one writing challenge a week for a year. More if you revisit prompts to try new ideas and angles featured in the guiding questions. Attribution is not required, but I will *happily promote* any published works people are willing to share as inspired by this book.

If you have trouble completing your own works, this is also a great way to create base notes for your writing coach, co-author or ghostwriter. As someone who works with dyslexic and ESL clients, I found this often makes life easier for both sides in the idea and planning stage of new projects.

This Book is for *Both* Hobby and Career Writers

Many, many writing prompt books out there are simply

writing and creativity exercises, and that is an awesome thing. However, I geared the prompts in this book toward novels and short stories. You can use them for fun, or you can use the final work for your writing career. They are designed for both!

Every Prompt is Engineered for Sci-Fi or Fantasy

The base idea *will* work for both genres and multiple settings, though you might need to swap a word here and there to fit your exact niche. The goal was to provide you with story seeds that could grow in as many directions as possible.

Are There Romance Prompts?

Yes and No. These prompts can be used with romantic elements. It is perfectly feasible to interject your romantic characters and their sub-plot into the larger story these are set to inspire. But as a head's up, there are no prompts specifically constructed as a romantic sci-fi or fantasy in this book. You will have to design and add those elements at your discretion.

Let's Go!

It is my fond hope this reference will be of great use to you. You are very welcome to email me requests and suggestions for future niche-specific story seed books as well! You'll find my contact info in the about author page at the end.

Let's get started! You can read through the prompts from start to finish or open to a random one. Happy plotting!

Prompt 1

A mysterious illness is spreading. In one season it has already decimated the local population, possibly other communities as well. What is worse, the protagonist (or someone they trusted) helped facilitate it.

- ❏ Who is the Protagonist? Will there be a definable Antagonist?

- ❏ Who will help or hinder the protagonist and antagonists as they reach toward their goals? Has the illness affected them? How are they still alive?

- ❏ When did the illness begin in relation to the start of the story?

- ❏ What are the symptoms?

- ❏ How was it made? How does it spread? Who originated it?

- ❏ Why was this illness released? Accident? Intentional? What was the original motivation?

- ❏ Where has it spread? Where will the story begin?

- ❏ What is a potentially fatal flaw for the Protagonist? What is a relatable or redeeming characteristic for the Antagonist?

Prompt 2

The protagonist is entrusted to be the diplomatic ambassador in attempted peace talks with a hostile country/planet/etc. However, their efforts meet constant opposition via culture clashes, opposition, riots, and even deadly attempts on their life.

- ❑ Describe the two cultures. Why do they clash so violently? Which one is the actual aggressor, if not both?

- ❑ What happened in history to make the two sides distrustful of each other?

- ❑ What do people from both side expect to gain from a peace agreement? Who would greatly benefit from the peace agreements failing?

- ❑ What tone do you want to set with each culture clash? What sort of clashes do you want to explore in the book? Are they resolved or steadily get worse?

- ❑ Where are the two cultures in relation to each other? Do they share a border? Are they on opposite ends of the world? How will the protagonist travel to the destination? Will the story open during the travel or straight into the strange land?

- ❑ Who is the Protagonist? How do they fit within their own culture? Who do they need to meet to get the talks underway? How are they perceived and treated?

- ❑ Will there be a definable Antagonist? What challenges besides the peace talks will the protagonist face? How will they overcome them? Will their mission ultimately succeed or fail?

Prompt 3

The Protagonist's (or Antagonist's/ Major Supporting Character's) family has searched for proof of an upcoming catastrophe for several generations. However, everyone sees their paranoia as a form of lunacy, and it has affected how they are viewed and treated... But they were right. So very right. Now the moment is at hand, and no one is prepared for it.

- ❏ What is the calamity? What formed the family's belief that it would happen? After several generations of being shunned and not taken seriously, how do they regard the people this calamity will affect?

- ❏ Who will it affect? What will the price be for the populace ignoring the signs? Is there anyone who wants the calamity to happen? What are their motivations?

- ❏ Is there a way to stop, escape, or mitigate the effects of the calamity? What will the protagonist have to do to stop it? What will they need? What key piece will they lack, and how do they need to acquire it? Will they succeed or fail?

- ❏ Is the Protagonist related to or close to the ones who have warned of the calamity? What was their belief or attitude before it became real? How do they feel now that the moment is at hand?

- ❏ Where will the story begin? Is this the same area the climactic scene will take place?

- ❏ The way the protagonist approaches the problem sets the plot, pace and tone. What sort of story will this be? A hero's journey? A race against time? A self-discovery? Eager hero or reluctant participant? What potentially fatal flaw do they have that could lead to complications or failure?

Prompt 4

The world is in chaos from a major climate crisis (a new ice age, thinning oxygen, a polar axis shift, etc). Mankind must adapt or die. But someone in the protagonist's group is trying to assure that doesn't happen.

- Is this a natural occurrence, or was human intervention involved?

- What are the people doing to adapt to or escape this changing environment? What resources are dying out? What is becoming vital for survival?

- How is the Protagonist and their family/team dealing with the crisis? Do they have access to resources they need or do they struggle to find basic necessities? Are there any critical issues they are dealing with like an illness or sudden loss of food supplies? Maybe they were separated in a journey?

- What is the primary goal of the Protagonist? What steps will they need to go through to reach this goal?

- Will the population ultimately adapt, escape, or die out? How will people as a whole change their behavior to fit this end situation? Which societal norms will be tested?

- What motivations would someone have to thwart survival? Who is their target? The protagonist specifically? A group? Mankind? What is their reasoning? What would make them assume they are doing the 'right' thing?

Prompt 5

The protagonist is trapped in a life they want no part of. There is better. They see it. Dream of it. They'd give anything for it. Now someone is offering that life on a silver platter- for a favor. But is the cost worth the prize?

- ❏ What sort of life is the Protagonist trapped in? Is it one people look down on? Ordinary? Is it one others assume would be wonderful and luxurious?

- ❏ Consider the core motivation. What is most desirable about the thing the protagonist wants? Why are they unable to attain it in their present condition? Make sure it is something that can convincingly drive the story. Is the motivator worth *anything*, even some moral grey areas, to attain?

- ❏ What sort of person would be capable of offering the protagonist what they want? Will they ultimately be supporters or Antagonists in the story?

- ❏ What favor will the benefactor ask? What is the cost of failing to fulfill their end of the bargain? What will the consequences be of *succeeding*?

- ❏ What parts of the setting will make this easier or harder for the Protagonist?

Prompt 6

A child of a high-ranking family was born with what would be considered a major defect in the world or society. They have gotten used to being treated differently as a 'spare' heir, and they had come to terms with their lot in life. But now they are suddenly heir apparent (or the new head of the family), and not everyone is happy about it.

- What defects could make the person look like an ill match for the role they are being thrust into? The 'defect' could be as simple as being born the wrong gender for traditions, or as complex as a genetic trait or lack of a specific essential talent.

- How does this defect affect their ability to perform their duties? Does it make diplomacy harder? Are there responsibilities that they have to improvise on? How much preparation was the 'spare' actually given up to this point?

- Will this person be the primary protagonist? Or will it follow someone closely affected by this person's new status shift? What POV will it be written from?

- How does the protagonist feel about this change in fate? How do people react to the sudden shift in status of an 'incompetent' leader?

- Who stands to gain from the sudden change? Who would gain from getting close to them?

Prompt 7

The protagonist is sent to a faraway land to join a colony established there. However, upon arrival, they find... nothing. The colony is totally deserted, but there are no apparent signs of an illness or attack. It is like the people simply vanished and left all their belongings behind. Worse, travel back is impossible for at least a few months (if ever).

- ❑ Who is with the protagonist? Do they have a means to communicate with anyone outside the colony? If they are alone, how do they deal with the loneliness?

- ❑ Is the surrounding area a paradise? Wasteland? Hostile? What sort of landmarks are nearby? What general climate and biome are they working with?

- ❑ Why did people settle out there? What sort of settlers were they? (examples: families? Explorers? Ex-convicts?) Did they come willingly or were they forced there? How long has the colony been there?

- ❑ It can be assumed some supplies are on-hand in the empty buildings, but how much? Is it adequate for all their needs until they can do something about the situation?

Prompt 8

The days are growing shorter and darker. Strange things lurk in the shadows that have never been seen before.

- ❑ Is this darkness a new occurrence, or something the protagonist is accustomed to?

- ❑ What is the cause of the shortening days? Does anyone in the story know, or is it a mystery? What sort of science, ideas, rumors, or lore do everyday people have about its origins?

- ❑ How do short days affect everyday life and the environmental setting? What challenges or benefits does it bring?

- ❑ Will these short days be a factor or the central focal point of the story? How will this darkness and the things lurking it it affect the story?

- ❑ What sort of creatures would thrive in the dark? Are they timid? pranksters? Hunters? How do they regard humans (or the protagonist's species)? Are they a boon or a threat to the protagonist's goals?

Prompt 9

Someone started taking a new medicine, and it changed them in a way that no one could have predicted.

- ☐ Who started taking the medicine? The protagonist? Someone close to them? The future antagonist?

- ☐ What were they taking the medicine for?

- ☐ What were the expected effects? What happened? How will this affect the larger story?

- ☐ Where will this take place in the story? The beginning? the backstory? Act 2? Near the end?

- ☐ How does the protagonist initially feel about the experimental treatment? How do they feel about the actual results? Does their view reflect how others see it?

- ☐ Conflict in opposition: If the medicine has a very good consequence, how would someone spin it as a threat? If the results are very bad- how would someone see it as a benefit to themselves or their agenda?

Prompt 10

He gave up the business after something happened that could not be undone. Now he might be the only one with an answer to the current crisis.

- ☐ Are they the protagonist, or someone the protagonist needs in order to fix the crisis?

- ☐ Do they actually know the answer? Or are very powerful (and potentially dangerous) figures just making that assumption?

- ☐ What is the current crisis? How does this person fit into its existence?

- ☐ Are there people who would want this person silenced? How far would they be willing to go to make sure no one solves the crisis? Bribery? Kidnapping? Murder? What motives would they have? Do they have good reasons but a bad plan? Are their reasons something that could pull an echo of pity from the reader? Or are they even the bad guy?? Maybe the protagonist blindly on the wrong side of the fight?

- ☐ Will the protagonist ultimately make things better or worse with the information? How will they ultimately deal with the crisis?

Prompt 11

A new disease (or its hastily made cure) is turning its recipients into monsters. Worse, there are signs that the outcome might have been premeditated.

- ❏ Where will the story start? At the hopeful start when people first hear about the cure? Right in the thick of the nightmare? Just after the first wave?

- ❏ Will the 'monster' traits be physical or psychological? What is the most terrifying part of the change?

- ❏ How will it affect how people with certain matching traits are treated by the population? Distrust? Violence? Isolation/Quarantine?

- ❏ How is this event affecting the protagonist and the people they are close to? How does it affect the population at large? What would someone wish to benefit from this?

- ❏ Is it curable or permanent? Contagious? What are the chances of immunity?

- ❏ Will it be the driving force in the story? Or one part of a much larger picture?

Prompt 12

The Protagonist's mentor has sent them to a major trade hub on a fairly routine mission. It turns out their mentor's reputation is 'interesting' to say the least. It causes the protagonist several problems that make the so-called errand much tougher than they bargained for.

- ❑ Think over the tone you want to set with the story. Will it be comical? Serious? Thrilling? Tragic?

- ❑ Think over the mentor. What are five words that would describe them? What sort of reputation would match these traits?

- ❑ What part of the hub are they on bad terms with? The Law? The underbelly? The ladies?

- ❑ Think up at least six problems this reputation would cause someone related to the mentor. Which three would drive a good story?

- ❑ Consider the relationship of the mentor and protagonist. Will the mentor become involved or let the protagonist suffer/grow from the experience? Do they have a history of doing this to the protagonist or is this highly unusual?

- ❑ Will it be the central story? Or will it be a major factor that acts as a catalyst to a larger and more complicated story?

Prompt 13

A pilgrimage that spans several generations is nearing an end. However, what awaits them is not what their predecessors expected at all.

- How many years/ generations did this pilgrimage span?

- Why did their predecessors start this journey? Was it voluntary?

- What keeps the later generations motivated to keep going? How do they feel being born into this journey? Happy? Resentful? Resigned?

- What is the reality waiting for them at the end?

- What parts of the culture were changed or lost in the practicalities of travel?

- Does the story start during the journey or right at the end?

- What trials and hardships are they about to face?

Prompt 14

A weapon (or other threat) that no one in the community has seen before has claimed a life.

- How does this weapon stand out from the weapons locals are familiar with?

- How does the community react as a whole? How do the individuals closest to the event see it?

- Every death should have a substantial impact on the story itself. What are the consequences of this particular death?

- Will this be a critical scene at the start, middle or finish of your story?

- What will be the main driving point of the story? The source of the weapon or the death itself?

Prompt 15

The answer to immortality has been found, but the cost is steep.

- ❑ How does immortality work in this story? Keep it *plausible* to your genre and setting.

- ❑ Who has access to immortality? One person? A community? A race? What are the advantages and consequences to this pool? Is it a cure or a curse?

- ❑ What is the cost to attain it? How is this cost dealt with?

- ❑ Who or what regulates it? Is it easily accessible or very limited?

- ❑ What significant figures are involved in your story?

- ❑ Is it a one-time fix? Or is it something that requires regular renewals?

- ❑ Is it part of the setting or a driving force in the story?

Prompt 16

Someone moves to a location with a very different culture from their own, and something is brewing in the shadows.

- Is the Protagonist the newcomer, or will they encounter the newcomer?

- What are the key differences between the two cultures that are about to clash?

- How long have they been there? Did they just step foot into this strange land? Or have they had enough time to find a shelter, job, etc? How do locals react to them?

- Will the newcomer trigger a great change in the community? Or will they get swept up in a larger plot due to timing?

- What themes will be explored as they progress in the story?

- Are they there voluntarily? Will the newcomer strive to integrate or rebel against the society they find themselves in?

Prompt 17

The story is told from the villain's point of view.

- ❑   To make the story compelling, the villains objective *must* be relatable in some way- if not the means to achieve it. What beliefs or redeeming qualities will they have to intrigue the reader?

- ❑   Will your end goal be to make the readers like or dislike the villain? Will their act of 'evil' be clear cut or in a moral grey area?

- ❑   Who will oppose them. How will you draw the reader to feel about them? Will they see the 'hero' as a good guy? Or as worse than the villain? Will they both be pitied for their inevitable battle?

- ❑   Traditionally, the villain is defeated at the end of the story. Is the villain destined to succeed or fail? What reactions will you wish to pull from the readers with this decision? Celebration? Sadness? Anger?

- ❑   What scenes will make the greatest impact in making readers feel the way you want to?

Prompt 18

A wish is granted and quickly regretted.

- ❑ Who attained the wish? The Protagonist? Someone they know? Someone dangerous?

- ❑ What is the nature of the wish?

- ❑ How was it granted? Supernatural means? A Favor? A bargain? An experiment? A chance opportunity?

- ❑ What are the consequences of having what they longed for?

- ❑ Will they need to reverse, overcome, or adapt to the changes this wish brings? What sort of scenes will drive this central idea forward?

Prompt 19

The instructions were simple. But sometimes the simplest requests are the one's hardest to follow.

- ❏ What is this instruction.

- ❏ What vital role does it play in the story? Is it a pivotal point? The central thing that drives the story? A main conflict for the protagonist? A catalyst to a much larger story?

- ❏ Who will obey or disobey it? What will motivate them to act as they do?

- ❏ What are the consequences (good or bad) if they are broken?

- ❏ Will the effects be a permanent feature in the story or 'fixable'?

Prompt 20

Something we perceive as infinite is becoming scarce (air, water, gravity, sunlight, fuel, etc.).

- Which abundant resource(s) are disappearing, and why?

- This sort of story requires some extensive research to make sure the reader will believe and follow the logic. Where will you draw your reference material and theories from?

- Who is suffering most from the crisis? How are they adjusting their lives to deal with the crisis?

- Who is profiting from it? How are they doing so? Selling the resources (or solutions)? A position of leadership? Hoarding for themselves? Rigging ways to steal the resource?

- How is the crisis affecting the protagonist and their community? What do they do about it initially? (Hide, gather, investigate, invent solutions, etc?)

- What is the breaking point that drives the story of the protagonist into action? What challenges will they face?

Prompt 21

They have a rare skill or trait that is more trouble than it is worth.

- What is the setting of your world? What is considered normal? What is the measurement of worth in society? What defines the powerful and the common?

- With the world above in mind, what sort of desired/taboo traits or skills would make the character stand out? Why? And what sort of problems would these skills bring with use?

- Is the protagonist the one with the skill? Or do they have significant interactions with the person?

- How does the skilled person deal with their skill or trait? Do they hide it? Show it off? Monetize it? Do they see it as a gift or a burden?

- How are they treated by society? Positive? Negative? Hunted? Revered?

- What are significant scenes you can use the skill/trait to develop story and character?

Prompt 22

It's not always the monsters we need to fear. Danger wears the face of what we trust.

- ❏ Make a list of things we tend to trust with little or no question. Which ones could drive an interesting story if exploited?

- ❏ How does this thing they trust leave a person vulnerable for what is to come?

- ❏ What is the motivation for the deception? How will it significantly drive your story to include it?

- ❏ Will the deception affect just the protagonist and company? Or an entire population? Will the protagonist be the deceiver?

- ❏ How quickly will the deception be revealed to the reader? What clues and red herrings will show up along the way?

- ❏ Will it succeed or fail in its goal in the story? What potential scenes would create the most impact on the reader?

Prompt 23

Quarantine has been broken, and it is a matter of time before the disease covers the entire territory.

- ❑ What form of disease will it be? An illness? Infection? A metamorphosis? Deadly to specific demographics?

- ❑ Prepare a list of resources to help you source and explain the illness in a way appropriate for your genre. What are some credible similar conditions you can use to design this disease?

- ❑ What are symptoms? How does it spread? How quickly is it spreading?

- ❑ Will the story focus on ending the disease or surviving it? How widespread is it by the time the story starts?

- ❑ What is your main protagonist in the story? A survivor? Infected? Someone who made the disease? Someone racing for a cure? What will drive them through the story?

- ❑ How are the people at large reacting to the disease? What will be some keys scenes in the story?

Prompt 24

The solution is at the top of the mountain. The trick is not dying on the way up.

- Alternative: What other location will you put the solution (and a major plot point) in the story?

- What problem is the protagonist trying to solve? Is it the primary problem? Or a challenge within a much larger issue?

- What skills and shortcomings will come into play for the protagonist (and team if applicable)?

- What will the setting be? What challenges will the setting bring? What dangers are in between them and their goal?

- Will they find what they seek at their destination? Or will it open a whole new line of problems?

Prompt 25

They were charged to protect someone, and now they are to blame for a death.

- ❑   Who will the protector be? The protagonist? The future antagonist? A major character?

- ❑   Was it the charge that died, or someone else? How does it affect the story? What chain of events will it trigger?

- ❑   Where in this timeline will the story begin? From whose point of view will it be told? What do they know (and what do they *think* they know) about the event?

- ❑   How will the protagonist be affected by the event? What challenges will they face as a result?

- ❑   How will the views of the protagonist *and reader* change in the course of the story? What elements will you need to add to create these changes at the right time?

Prompt 26

Artificial enhancements are all the rage. However, something is being added to these enhancements that no one bargained for.

- What are the enhancements in question? Is it appearances? An attribute? Intelligence? A link others (like telepathy or internet)? A 'larger than life' ability?

- What do these enhancements give the person that attains them? New access to something exclusive? Prestige? A desired goal?

- Is the enhancement popular because it is rare? Or because *everyone* else has them?

- What is being added to the enhancement? Is it intentional or an unforeseen circumstance? Do developers reveal the situation or keep it hidden? What is their motivation?

- Do the main characters have these enhancements? What are their attitudes and beliefs regarding them? What events will change or reinforce those beliefs?

- How will the enhancements drive the story, and how will you ultimately wish the reader to feel about artificially enhancements vs Nature?

Prompt 27

It's for the greater good, but at what cost?

- ❑ List out a series of things that are normally 'wrong' (ex: sealing someone in a room with a fire), and then at least three ways it can be considered the 'right thing' (ex: saving the rest of the ship). Which ones would provoke a strong story and critical thought?

- ❑ Will this controversy happen before, during, or at the climatic point of the story? How will it have a significant role in character and plot development?

- ❑ What events or factors will make this choice hard yet inevitable?

- ❑ Will it be the primary protagonist or antagonist doing this thing? Will you ultimately have the readers support, sympathize with, or denounce the act and resulting chain of events? What plot elements will you need to create this reaction?

- ❑ What will the gains be? What will be the consequences? How will it change various characters in the story as a result.

Prompt 28

The prize in this game is worth killing for.

- ❑ How dangerous is the game? Can or will people actually die, or will it just seem that intense?

- ❑ What is the prize? Why is it so significant to this world? Is it a limited resource? A tangible prize? Prestige? Entry to an exclusive place?

- ❑ How many contestants can win the prize? How many are competing? How many does the story follow?

- ❑ Write a brief description of each character followed, and a one sentence description of the major characters they will interact with.

- ❑ What will some of the rules and penalties be in the game? How involved are the judges? Which characters from above will thrive or struggle under the rules? (If none would struggle, reevaluate your character diversity).

- ❑ What events will affect the progress and outcome of the story? Will there be any cheating? Sabotage? Accidents?

Prompt 29

The land is inhospitable. But they can never return to where they came from.

- Is it an individual? A group? A community? Why are they unable to backtrack?

- Are they there to settle or pass through? Why was this place chosen despite the dangers?

- What makes this place inhospitable? What challenges will will affect their goals and survival?

- What skills do they have that give them an edge? What skills do they lack that they must compensate for?

- What other factors will contribute to the story? What takeaway will readers come away with?

Prompt 30

They are forced into an alliance with someone they consider an enemy.

- Will 'they' be individuals? Groups? Races? What divides to the point of being enemies?

- What event would be dire enough to throw two opposing sides into a temporary alliance?

- What are some challenges that will inevitably arise from their opposing viewpoints?

- Will they reconcile their differences or just work around them until the major conflict is resolved? Will they manage to overcome the various trial in the process?

- What messages or takeaways will the characters (and readers) walk away with?

Prompt 31

A stranger who seems to know the protagonist well demands that they follow them to somewhere suspicious/dangerous.

- ❑ What is the protagonist like? How would they realistically react to a stranger asking them to go somewhere outside their comfort zone?

- ❑ What is the setting? What sights, smells, etc will set the tone you are looking for?

- ❑ What happens if they follow? What happens if they don't? Which will contribute to the pace and development of the story?

- ❑ What series of events will their decision trigger? How will they affect the larger story?

- ❑ Who is the stranger? Why do they target the protagonist? What do they expect to gain from their compliance? What forced their hand to make such a suspicious demand?

Prompt 32

A renowned figure found a way to make certain animals as cognitive as humans.

- How did they do it? What was their purpose for doing so? Was it the primary objective or a side effect?

- What creature(s) have been given human-like cognisance? What natural behaviors and instincts will interact with their newfound intellect?

- If unchecked, how will it affect humans (or the equivalent race in story) in the short term? How will it reshape the world in a year? Decade? Century?

- With the above three points in mind, where in the timeline will your story begin? During the creation or sometime after? How will the landscape and culture look at this point?

- How does the protag view the creatures? Were they involved with the project? Oppose it? A civilian/Bystander? How were their lives changed by this artificial evolution?

- What conflicts will arise in the story?

Prompt 33

All technology (or powers, magic, power sources, etc) has suddenly failed all at once. None work whatsoever. And someone is very content with that fact.

- How disruptive is this to everyday life for the affected population? How about for the protagonist's life?

- Will the story start before the 'crisis' begins? Right after? Some weeks later? Generations later?

- What series of events led to this situation? Who or what ultimately caused it?

- Is the loss of technology (magic, etc) inconvenient? Disastrous? Life and death? How do people adapt and fail to adapt? Can it be fixed, or is it permanent?

- Who gains from this failure? How will they capitalize on it? Who suffers the worst from the loss?

- What problems and unexpected advantages does the protagonist gain from the situation?

Prompt 34

Without fail, their predictions become real. Are they foretelling the future or crafting it? Either way, their latest divination affects the protagonist directly.

- ❑ Is it a good or bad future? What are the details? Is it clear or cryptic?

- ❑ Who is it for, and how does it affect the protagonist? Who will oppose this prophecy, and who will work toward its success?

- ❑ The age old question: Is fate fixed or a product of choice? How will the answer work its way into the story?

- ❑ How does the figure/organization predict the future so accurately? Are they using hard data? Ai's? Are they self-fulfilling? Magic? A manufactured con-artistry?

- ❑ Will the protagonist be struggling to defy the future or make it a reality? What challenges will they face? Who else will be affected?

Prompt 35

The days are getting darker, and the nights are growing eerily silent. Something hides in this dark that they can't afford to ignore.

- ❑ Are the dark days literal or figurative? What are the signs that something is wrong and unnatural about the situation?

- ❑ What dangers does the darkness bring? Who does it affect the most?

- ❑ What forces the protagonist's hand in dealing with it?

- ❑ Is it a problem that can be fixed? Or must it be survived, endured, escaped, etc?

- ❑ Is it more dangerous to live with the danger or to oppose it?

- ❑ How do various characters adapt? Which ways of handling the situation are good? Unhealthy? Deadly?

Prompt 36

Immortality is no longer a myth. But it comes at a great cost.

- Is the "Immortality Factor" a new discovery, or has it been around for a while?

- How is it achieved? Who has access to it? Is it a one-time thing? Or does it have to be refreshed now and then? Can it be *undone*?

- Is the immortality all-encompassing? Or does it affect only very certain factors like illness or aging?

- What are the good things that this form of immortality can bring? What are the distinct drawbacks?

- What is the protagonist's view on immortality? The antagonist? Major characters? How do their collective views drive the story and various conflicts forward?

Prompt 37

The place is a trap. Complete with bait to lure the unsuspecting in. Now if they don't escape, the consequences could be dire.

- What is this trap? A building? An establishment? Community? Game area? A whole planet?

- What is this place designed to catch? What does it use to lure the intended target(s) in?

- Who or what is using the trap to their advantage? Why?

- How does one escape the trap? Do characters involved know this? Or will it be revealed in the story? Will it be explained outright or via unintentional clues/signs?

- Is it worse to stay in the trap or to try to escape it?

- What sorts of things will be encountered inside? What physical and psychological threats are present.

Prompt 38

They are mirror images of each other. And one copy is trying to steal the life of the other.

- ❏ Which one is the "copy?" A jealous twin? A Doppleganger? Shapeshifter? Con artist? Clone? Cyborg?

- ❏ Whose point of view will the story be told from? Original? Copy? Maybe a character close to one of them?

- ❏ Why does the copy want the other's identity? How far will they go? Will they succeed, fail, or have mixed results?

- ❏ What events will the protagonist face in this scenario? What challenges will they endure? Will they encounter failure or setbacks?

- ❏ Who ultimately wins in the bigger picture? Original? Copy? Or someone else entirely?

Prompt 39

They came to the land bearing gifts and miracles. But what is the hidden motive of their generosity?

- ❑ Who do the gift bearers target? What is their motive? At what point in the story will it be revealed?

- ❑ Whose point of view is best suited for this scenario? How do they view the situation?

- ❑ What sort of misunderstandings and assumptions can drive the conflict?

- ❑ What sort of gifts and miracles do they bring? What human emotions do they appeal to? Safety? Greed? Longevity?

- ❑ How do people react? What positive and negative human behaviors appear? How do they react when/if the real motive is revealed?

Prompt 40

They can go into places most other people don't... or can't. Even places they shouldn't go. And the consequences of treading in forbidden places can be dire if they are caught.

- ☐ Who are they? Is this mode of travel and entry paranormal or skill based?

- ☐ What sorts of places can they get into? Why can they do this while others can't?

- ☐ What are the obvious consequences if they get caught? What are some less obvious consequences that they might not think about?

- ☐ How will it affect their relationships with others? Their community? Family? Authorities? Etc.

- ☐ What would motivate them to use this ability?

- ☐ Where did they attain this ability? Is it well known? A secret? A fluke? Do the users see it as a curse, a gift, or a tool?

- ☐ What series of events will using this ability at the wrong time trigger in the story?

Prompt 41

The ceremony must always be done to the letter. Always. But the true reason has been long lost in a sea of myths and legends. Now the ritual is broken.

- ☐ What is the reason for the ritual? How will it fit into the rest of the setting?

- ☐ What do people in the current day think the consequences of breaking the ritual are? What are the true consequences?

- ☐ What are the steps to the ritual? Which parts are the most vulnerable to mistakes or willful deviations?

- ☐ Is the story about actively breaking the ritual? Surviving the aftereffects? Fixing it?

- ☐ Who breaks the ritual in the story? What are their motives?

- ☐ How will breaking the ritual affect the setting and story at large?

Prompt 42

The end of an Age has come. They must pick themselves up from the ashes with one central law: SURVIVE.

- ☐ How expansive is this upheaval? Does it affect a single person? A community? A territory? The world? Multiple worlds?

- ☐ Who or what turned their existence on its ear? How?

- ☐ List out 3-5 survivors and their back stories. Which one(s) will your story follow? What point of view will be used?

- ☐ What challenges will they face? What factors make survival less certain? What details will the reader know that the characters will be ignorant of?

- ☐ What parallel stories will run in this world aside from survival?

Prompt 43

A monster has taken up residence, and it has the inhabitants in terror. Someone must deal with this, but one wrong move could make things worse.

- ☐ Is the monster a literal one? Or a person/creature that operates at a terrifying level? What will you base their physiology and behaviors on?

- ☐ What is more terrifying? The monster itself or how certain people use its presence to their benefit?

- ☐ Why is the monster here? What makes them haunt this place vs another? What keeps them here?

- ☐ Does the monster's behavior lend credit to the local fears? Or is it simply their presence that has people terrified? What do they do (and not do) to lend credit to their reputation?

- ☐ Is the protagonist a traditional hero? A hunter? A citizen? A con-artists? What strengths do they have to deal with this issue? What weaknesses do they have that could end up their downfall?

- ☐ What red herrings and plot twists can you throw at the readers to keep the story thrilling and unpredictable for the readers?

Prompt 44

The construct is so advanced that it seems almost sentient. But it does not understand human frailty. Only its "programming."

- ☐ What is the sentient construct? A device? A robot/golem? A building or ship perhaps? Was it created with science or magic ...or a mix? What gave it this near-human level of sentience?

- ☐ How is our current technology similar? What are the super human advantages? What are the limitations of artificial intelligence?

- ☐ Why was it created? What events led up to its concept and creation? What was it made to do?

- ☐ What issues arise in its programming? What loopholes and special circumstances could prove problematic?

- ☐ What event will trigger a chain of events in this story? What central themes will the interactions between construct and mankind be explore?

- ☐ How can it be beneficial? How can it be dangerous? How will these aspects drive a story?

Prompt 45

They must hide in plain sight, but discovery is death- or worse.

☐   What sort of theme will you focus on relating to this deception? Will it focus on the pretense (example: Accepting yourself as you are)? Or around a larger story (example: The sacrifices made to avenge a wrong)? How will this theme affect the story? What will be the final resolution or takeaway for the reader?

☐   Who or what are they? Why do they have to hide their true identity? What series of events led to this situation?

☐   Is it basic survival, or is there a specific goal they cannot achieve in their own identity? What rewards, consequences, and dangers are present for pretending to be something they are not?

☐   What do they have to do in order to conceal themselves? How is it effective? What are the weak points?

☐   Who knows (or will find out) their real identity? What will be their motivation to reveal or help them conceal this deception? How would each relationship have differed if there was no deception?

Prompt 46

Their words are like honey, but their plans are anything but sweet— and someone is hopelessly ensnared.

- ☐ Who or what is the well-spoken person? What logic or promises are they offering to convince someone to act? What is their goal?

- ☐ What is the apparent reward to taking them up on their offering?

- ☐ What is the apparent cost to listening to their message? How does the person pay it?

- ☐ What are the hidden costs and consequences? Will they be revealed to the reader right away or as a plot twist?

- ☐ Point of view: Who will tell the story? The victim? The promise makers? A third party?

- ☐ What factors contribute to their victim taking the offer? For example, a recent crisis or a personality trait.

- ☐ Will the victim ultimately be saved or lost in the promise?

- ☐ What sort of message do you want readers to ponder by reading this story?

Prompt 47

A creature long thought to be a myth is right in front of them. However, not all stories are true.

- ☐ What person or creature will you use in the story? What details will validate their existence to readers? Are they peaceable? Vicious? Hunters?

- ☐ What myths are there regarding this creature in your setting? Which ones are correct, half-correct, and outright wrong?

- ☐ How do the myths affect how the people in the story react and interact with them? What are the consequences of relying on the wrong myths?

- ☐ Why have they appeared? Why do people *think* they appeared? Are there any opportunities for character or plot conflict?

- ☐ People react to things in different ways. What are some ways characters will react to the creatures and new circumstances? What does their existence mean for the people involved?

- ☐ Point of View: Will the story take place from the creature's point of view, or the ones who discovered them?

Prompt 48

Years ago, leading experts suddenly vanished without a trace. Now everyone is about to find out why.

- ☐ What were they experts of? How did their loss affect the greater community?

- ☐ Was it voluntary or were they spirited away against their will? Are they currently alive and well?

- ☐ Are there any survivors or people rising to replace them—and how?

- ☐ What was the reason behind their disappearance? What goals and motivating factors caused the sudden disappearance?

- ☐ Does someone reveal the reason behind it? Or will a character stumble into the answer? At what point in the story will it be revealed in full?

- ☐ What conflicts does this situation open your story up to?

Prompt 49

Attaining this resource is a matter of life and death- but someone may have to die to attain it.

- ☐ What is the resource? Is it a common basic need in scarce supply? An ingredient for a cure? A super rare substance?

- ☐ What are the risks of not attaining this resource? What are the dangers people will face trying to attain it?

- ☐ How large a group is needed to attain the resource? A few people? An army? What skills, knowledge, traits, or luck do they need to be successful?

- ☐ What are the deadly risks that could kill someone in trying to attain it? Why is it worth the risk? Does anyone disagree?

- ☐ Who or what will oppose success in attaining it? Whose point of view will the story be told from? How does it affect how the story unfolds?

Prompt 50

They ruined their credibility. Now no one is listening to them when a real crisis is about to hit.

- ☐ Will the story be told by the person, or someone who hears their warnings?

- ☐ What did they say or do to be automatically discredited now?

- ☐ What is the current situation, and why is it so unbelievable? Why are they the only ones able to see it?

- ☐ How far off is the crisis? And at what point will the story start? Before the discovery? Long after? Right as the situation begins?

- ☐ Do they convince anyone, or do they have to handle the situation on their own? What is their usual method for handling each challenge amid the disbelief?

- ☐ How are they affected emotionally, socially, and mentally by the lack of belief and support?

- ☐ Will they ultimately stop the crisis? Lead story into evading or surviving it? Or will they contribute to the crisis in spite?

Prompt 51

They have never stepped foot in this place. Now that they have, everything they know has changed.

- ☐ What is the place? Is it small like a room? A community? An entire world or reality?

- ☐ Who is stepping in? A person? A group? A community?

- ☐ Why have they never stepped foot in this place before? Why are they doing so now?

- ☐ What did they expect? What did they find instead?

- ☐ How will this place change them? Will it be a perception? A belief pattern? With it hurt or help them as a person?

- ☐ What sort of challenges will they be prepared for? What will they be vastly unprepared for? How will they grow or devolve as they interact with this place?

- ☐ Will they ultimately keep a connection to this place or strive to close the entryway again? Why?

Prompt 52

They escaped to pursue their paradise. But it's not at all what they thought it would be.

- ☐ Who are they? Are they a single person or a group?

- ☐ What is their current situation like? What are the risks of leaving it?

- ☐ What is this paradise? Why do they see it as such?

- ☐ What ultimately motivates them to make the journey? What challenges do they face? Is it worth the risk in effort? Or do they find themselves in a worse situation than they began?

- ☐ How did they hear about it? Why did that source share the information? Was any misinformation accidental or on purpose?

- ☐ How is their paradise different from what they heard? Is it apparent right away? Or is it more subtle and revealed over time?

- ☐ How do they react when their ideals meet reality? How will it motivate them in plot and character growth?

Conclusion

I'm happy you browsed through this brainstorming reference. Hopefully you found a few ideas that really resonated!

On the following pages, you'll find a few resources that will be helpful on your next step. Whether you keep them as creative exercises or strive to create a finished publication- I wish you all the best!

If you have ideas, feedback, or suggestions for future publications, I'd love to hear from you. Please feel free to visit my website or shoot me an e-mail anytime.

May the words flow swiftly and freely!

All the best,

Shandee
www.nisfreelance.com

My Top Ten Favorite Sci-fi and Fantasy

I am a true believer in the idea that you have to be a good reader in order to be a good writer. One of the best ways to write sci-fi or fantasy fiction is to look at what appeals to readers and why.

Here is a list of some of my personal all-time favorite readings in the genres. I highly recommend making a similar list for your greats to get a feel for what resonates best with you as well. You can find more trends and lists at sites like Goodreads.

1. **The Pern Series by Anne McCaffrey.** While it could drudge on in spots, the world building of Anne McCaffrey has always intrigued me. It was a touch science fiction meeting a world that forgot its high-tech ways as it colonized and lived with the planet's version of dragons. Each book was a standalone, but they also wove in elements and history from prior stories to make a far larger tapestry.

2. **The Orc Queen Trilogy by Morgan Howell**. My absolute favorite part of this book series is how the reader kept all the orc stereotypes at the start- but as the story progressed each one was given a very good reason. By the time you finish the third book, the orcs are a civilized race (tropes and all) while the humans are barbaric and monstrous. Add in great story-weaving and wordsmithing, and it made for a story I was sad to see end.

3. **The Name of the Wind by Patrick Rothfuss**. The protagonist is one of the best antiheroes I have seen written. He is an underdog with a photographic memory and a keen wit. He is not the typical hero. He cheats. He breaks into forbidden rooms and rivals' quarters. He pulls pranks and breaks rules-- and every time he legitimately gets ahead those former questionable actions sends him two steps back. My favorite part of the series is how the author takes every trope and predictable outcome-- and turns them *completely on their ear* with reasonable but delightfully unpredictable twists.

4. **The Tapestry Book 1 by Henry H Neff**. It is a very Harry Potter-like story. Kid plucked from the world of the mundane and attends a magic school. Magic creatures all over. An evil force targeting said school and its students. However, this one introduces the danger and suspense much earlier on than the more familiar wizarding universe. Plus, it weaves in a lot more history and real-world myths in the process.

5. **The Postman by David Brin**. My favorite part about this book is the hero is not some rugged warrior or hunter braving the wastelands of a post-apocalyptic world. It's about a common survivor that sparks hope of a whole region with a lie and people's desperate need for connection to others. A guy in a scavenged post office jacket gets drawn into a story he couldn't have begun to anticipate. It is proof that your protagonist does not need to be the best to make a memorable story.

6. **Dark Apostle by Anthony Reynolds**. This book was *dark*, which is not something I normally go for. However, the story brought out horror. It made war ugly and terrifying. It drew out the despair of a one-sided battle. I loved and hated every second simply because it could pull out emotions that many writers are hesitant to fully explore. Plus, it threw the typical tropes to the wind with the cold fact that the heroes aren't always good people, and they don't always win.

7. **Storm Front by Jim Butcher**. To be frank, the author is brilliant at pacing. They can strike up the exact right balance of seriousness and dry humor to keep me engaged. They break up the action with just enough downtime to develop future scenes. And the talking skull is one of the best supporting sidekicks I've read recently. I had a harder time getting into the second and third books given it felt like the author was trying too hard on the magical aspects, but the first was a definite favorite.

8. **Aliens vs Predator: Prey by Steve and Stephanie Perry**. This was not just world building. It was the building of culture, psychology, technology, and more of three different alien races plus the way these things interacted and clashed with one another on a planet not their own. More importantly: When I saw the cover over ten years later, it triggered a rush of excitement and a desire to re-read it. That's the kind of staying power a writer wants for their books.

9. **Forging of the Darksword by Margaret Weis and Tracy Hickman**. A world where magic determines who you will be and infects every aspect of life. To be born without magic, as the anti-hero protagonist, is a death sentence. The story was a bit wordy and slow to start, but it made it up with a whole world and supporting cast to get to know.

10. **The Alien Chronicles by Deborah Chester**. While the title implies a sci-fi, I'll dub it a high-tech space fantasy, given many tropes but very little science comes into play. This work is another that thrilled me when I spied it many years after reading it cover to cover on restless nights. I was fascinated with the setting, the characters in their complex variety, and subtle parallels to a very old but well-known story of a man raised with the royal heir that would one day be a bitter rival.

As one reads through this list, it is easy to see certain repeating themes of well thought out worlds, unusual twists, and complex casts of characters. It would be reasonable to say any story I write would reflect these features. Those would be a part of my voice.

With that, I highly encourage you to also create your own Top 10 List. Then describe exactly what put it there. With this exercise, you can find out small details about your written tastes that you didn't even know you had!

Recommended Resources:

Ready to take your idea to the next level? Here are a few things you should consider adding to your writer's toolbox:

Outlining Your Novel Workbook by K.M. Weiland: A very detailed workbook that you can use to flesh out your idea into a full detailed outline.

The Writers Helping Writers Thesaurus Series by Angela Ackerman and Becca Puglisi: A series of specialized thesauruses just for emotions, character traits, settings and more. Not only do they go over fresh words to use- they go over things that affect each listing. For example, in their negative trait thesaurus, if you look under "Indecisive" you will find associated behaviors and attitudes that you can write into the scene, some possible causes, how indecisiveness can be a good or bad thing, and how to overcome it as a major flaw.

The Writer's Market: A book compilation of *thousands* of publishing companies based on genres, length, niches and more. If you plan to publish your final work, you can easily find dozens of places to submit it to, along with some average prices, royalties and where to find submission guidelines.

Scrivener: I can not get myself to use this, admittedly. I am a physical notebook and pen person. However, it is an excellent way for many people to organize and write out their first drafts. You can get a special 30 "working" day trial on their host website. They only count the 30 days you use the program, not the traditional 30 consecutive days.

Hemmingway Editor: A great resource for checking each chapter for redundancy, passive sentences, poor word choices, and readability score (You want it about a 6 or 7 for general audiences). The browser version is free to use, and the offline version is a flat one-time fee.

Grammarly: The premium version is one of the most advanced checkers on the market. It also has a browser extension that will check your emails, forum posts, and more as you self-market or prepare to send in a pitch to a publisher.

Canva: A great site for beginners to make simple book covers, social media images, letterheads, banners and more. The drag and drop tech is very user friendly. Just make sure you use CC0 Free images from places like Pixabay and Unsplash or pay the proper fees for the intended use. If you do use one of Canva's premium images, make sure you read over the limits and permissions.

About The Author

Shandee Niswander

Shandee is a ghostwriter and copywriter that strives to people achieve their content goals. Nothing is impossible! You just need the information or opportunity to make that first step.

Shandee believes that you cannot effectively write about life without being a part of it. As a result, she makes time to be an active part of her community, from attending a weekly friendship club to volunteer work at her local community center.

**Visit me on
NisFreelance.com
to learn more**

OTHER BOOKS BY SHANDEE NIS

This is my debut publication. Hooray!

Coming in 2020

Story Seeds: Horror Edition

Blog Content Accelerators: Natural Health Edition

Copywriting Tips: Pro Moves to Better Content

LEAVE ME A REVIEW!

If you enjoyed this book or found it useful, please take a moment to leave a review on Amazon. I'm always interested in learning what you like, think and want. I read all the reviews personally.

Thank you for your support!